UNSTUCK
for WORDS

HOW TO START & FINISH
ANY WRITING PROJECT

First printing errata — page 12
The practical writing tips section begins on page 45
and grammar quiz section begins on page 48.

A 10-step, easy-to-follow guide to quick, creative & logical writing

Leon Linderman and Judy Goldwasser

Manufactured in the United States of America

1997   1996   1995   1994   6   5   4   3   2   1

Illustrations by Linda Marie Stevens.

Published by:
Writing Dynamics
346 W. Cambourne
Ferndale, Michigan 48220
810-543-3392

Distributed by:
Cedar Bend Press,Ltd.
3578 Larchmont
Ann Arbor, Michigan 48105
313-995-0722

ISBN 0-9638780-0-X

Contents

"This short program guides the writer's thinking through ten easy steps to a meaningful, organized and clear product."

— Rowena M. Wilhelm, PhD.,

former director, Reading and Learning Skills Center, University of Michigan

"In **Unstuck for Words,** *Goldwasser and Linderman offer valuable guidelines on using the English language competently and persuasively. An effective resource for anyone who has faced the task of writing quickly and well."*

— John Klemme,

English Department Chair, Groves High School, Beverly Hills, Michigan

Foreword

Several readings of this wise and wonderful little book have confirmed my first impression: it is hard to imagine a more useful or complete guide to writing good, clear English.

This book is for everybody who wants to be proficient in writing: high school, college or graduate students facing the dread blank page; business people who must produce good memos, letters or speeches; accountants and engineers, often too jargon-heavy in their writing; and even professional journalists.

It is a natural for high school and college composition classes, though one of its great virtues — a highly practical, unpedantic approach — may turn off some academicians.

Unstuck for Words shows the way to clear, effective writing in a series of logical steps, presented in the clean and lively style its authors recommend. It offers a strong antidote to fear of writing, a phobia that afflicts people in all walks of life.

Calculated to instill confidence, it addresses two common fears:

1) Fear about our ability to define exactly what we want to say and where to start;

2) Fear that we will embarrass ourselves with incorrect grammar and spelling.

Unstuck addresses the first fear by acknowledging that we must think clearly before we can write clearly. But the book stresses that such thinking does not require great talent or intellect. It demands only some effort plus a technique the authors thoughtfully provide.

The authors have also come up with an ingenious and highly effective approach to the "grammar block." They reason that most of their readers have gone through at least the eighth grade and therefore have the basic language skills they need to become good writers. People should write as they talk and plunge into writing uninhibited by grammar and spelling concerns. They can always use a last-minute computer spell-check or a good proofreading to clear up the mechanical details.

Goldwasser and Linderman clearly set forth all of the major elements of any writing task while wisely avoiding academic or rigid approaches. The drudgery of preparing a formal outline, for instance, can stifle the impulse and ability to write clean, easy prose. *Unstuck* provides an effective way to avoid such an outline.

In easy-to-follow steps, with illustrative examples, this book shows how to break down any subject into its component parts and how to put those parts together in logical order. Those who master the technique in simpler forms — brief letters or memos — can apply it to more complex efforts, much as the mason builds a cathedral, one stone at a time.

Unstuck ends with a section identifying the most common crimes against good English usage — the number is surprisingly small — and shows exactly how to correct them without dragging us through the academics of grammar and syntax.

Take one of the most common grammatical errors: "John took Mary and I out to dinner," or, even worse, "took she and I." Somehow, the accusative "me" has come to be less refined than the nominative "I." *Unstuck* shows how always to make the right choice without studying declensions and cases: simply drop Mary (or she), and you're left with "John took I to dinner." Any questions? Let's never make that mistake again.

All of a sudden, with this book as a guide, the work of writing becomes a lot less scary. That is a great gift to the many would-be writers who will be fortunate enough to find and read *Unstuck for Words*.

Throughout my career, I have worked with other writers to improve their skills and have always tried to improve my own. I regret that I didn't have this little book to help me do it.

William H. Schoen

(William H. Schoen has a lifetime of experience writing speeches, articles and presentations in private industry, as manager of Editorial Services at Ford Motor Company, and government, as a White House and State Department speechwriter.)

Preface

Education, career expertise, even intelligence don't necessarily translate into writing skills.

I became acutely aware of that observation several years ago when I realized how many of my fellow members in the Greater Detroit Chapter of the American Society for Training and Development (ASTD) were struggling when it came time to commit their programs to paper. My colleagues had the advantage of fine educations and were well-versed in their fields. But for many of them, writing was painstakingly slow and often it did not turn out the way they wanted it to.

Responding to this need, I began a collaborative Writers Special Interest Group as an information and support group for members who wished to enhance their writing skills and even publish their work. Input from group members intersected with my own lifelong fascination with the writing process; *Unstuck for Words* began to crystalize.

As the book took shape in my head, the Writers Special Interest Group provided an unexpected benefit: I met my co-author, Judy Goldwasser. I quickly observed Judy's passion for helping people write as simply and as clearly as she does. It was the beginning of a professional relationship that led to our collaboration on *Unstuck for Words*.

Judy and I are thrilled that our 10-step technique will now reach a much larger audience. We know that people who use our book will find that writing effectively and persuasively becomes easier and more enjoyable than they ever imagined. We couldn't ask for a better reward for our efforts.

Leon Linderman

Acknowledgments

Special thanks to the many members of the Writers Special Interest Group of the Greater Detroit Chapter of the American Society for Training and Development who offered suggestions and encouragement.

Leon Linderman

With appreciation for my first editor at the *Detroit Free Press*, Tom Wark, whose skill I'll always admire but never match, and my husband, Jim, who taught me what it's like to live with a writer.

Judy Goldwasser

Every Time You Write, You Face Two Dilemmas

1 How to be creative without sacrificing logic and clarity and

2 How to complete your project within a limited time period.

Often, the challenge seems overwhelming. You don't know *where* to begin, and you don't know *how* to begin. This book is designed to show you how to start and successfully finish any writing project that comes your way. It is user-friendly, compact and easy to follow. We think it will prove a welcome relief from the much longer and far more tedious instructional books now on the market.

It won't take long before writing, a problem for most people, becomes an opportunity for you.

Why You Need This Book

Good writing is neither magical nor mysterious. It is simply another way of talking.

But millions of bright, articulate people have convinced themselves that they simply can't write. Chances are you are one of them. Talking is not a problem. But the moment you have to put words on paper, your confidence fades.

What you probably don't realize is that you really can write. In fact, you most likely learned everything you need to know about writing by the sixth grade. *Unstuck for Words* is not another grammar book. What it offers are ten simple steps to shape what you already know into concise, effective prose.

The tools work equally well for any writing — from a brief office memo to lengthy technical reports to a book-length manuscript.

In fact, think of *Unstuck for Words* as a toolbox filled with tools for effective writing. You will learn how to use and feel comfortable with each tool in the box. Most likely, you will not need every tool for every job, but you must be familiar with each of them and know that they will all be there when you need them.

How To Use This Book:

To use *Unstuck for Words* most effectively, don't try to cover the entire book at once. Take one step at a time until you feel comfortable with it. Follow the examples, and ask yourself how they apply to your writing. When you've completed all ten steps, read the practical writing tips that follow (Page 15). Then test yourself on the grammar quiz (Page 19) and check your answers. Make sure you understand each grammatical point. Once you do, you're guaranteed to be ahead of almost everyone else.

After you've worked through the *Unstuck for Words* writing example, choose a writing project of your own. Follow it through each of the ten *Unstuck for Words* writing steps. When you've finished, reread the *Unstuck for Words* practical writing tips and apply them to what you've just written. Finally, check your final product against the *Unstuck for Words* grammar guidelines. Before long, you'll find yourself moving from step to step without even looking at the book — and you'll wonder why you ever said you couldn't write.

You're almost ready to start — and finish successfully — your first writing project with this book as your guide. First, however, you must know how to use your head . . .

Using Your Head

Or How To Make An Opportunity Out Of A Problem

The human brain has two sides. When it comes to writing, each side functions separately but plays an equally important role. The right side is creative. It is responsible for generating the ideas that you will eventually put on paper. The left side is logical. It makes sure that you express those ideas by using the correct words in understandable patterns.

Writing well involves a balancing act. If you don't coordinate both sides, your writing will be either so mechanical it lacks originality or so creative it lacks clarity.

In school, most of us developed the logical side of our brains. Our grades depended more on being correct than on being creative.

Now, as adults, we have jobs that require us to write quickly and logically. The committee needs the agenda memo today, and the boss wants the training report yesterday.

In our haste to get these reports down on paper, we often restrict or eliminate input from the creative side of our brains. The ideas cease to flow, and we run into problems. We may be totally unable to write, a state commonly known as writer's block, or we may fall back on ineffective language and cliche-ridden ideas.

The purpose of this book is to show you how to unite creativity and logic in a writing style that is comfortable to you and persuasive to others. You'll learn to use the same techniques as professional writers through practical examples and practice exercises. As a result, you'll improve your writing and increase your speed.

As you work, keep in mind that it's always helpful to divide the writing process into two parts:

1 First, concentrate on getting your words on paper.

2 Then, worry about getting them right. With this in mind, you can now begin by learning to mind-map.

Mind Mapping

Most likely, when you were a student, your teachers told you always to begin writing with an outline. But outlines depend too much on logic and organization — and too little on creativity and originality. There is a much easier and more effective approach to starting any writing. It's called mind-mapping. Mind-mapping is valuable because it engages all of your brainpower, including the creative side that generates new ideas. It expands, rather than narrows, your options.

To practice mind-mapping, take an 8 1/2-by-11-inch piece of blank paper. Eliminate distractions by clearing your desk of everything but the paper, a pen or pencil,and a highlighter. You're now ready to mind-map:

STEP 1: Ask yourself what you want to say. Why are you writing the report or memo in the first place? Once you decide your reason for writing, state it as briefly as possible.

Pretend someone is running out the door and says, "I'm late. You have just 15 seconds to tell me..."

Here are some sample statements:
- "We need a new piece of equipment."
- "We must improve customer service."
- "Too many people are showing up late for meetings."

STEP 2: Write your statement in the middle of a sheet of paper and draw a circle around it.
This is your core idea or topic statement (Figure A).

STEP 3: Determine your audience.
It may be your boss, a subordinate or a group such as a committee. Then name your target audience on the paper beneath your core idea (Figure B). Keep that audience in mind as you formulate your ideas and put them on paper.

> **Tip: If you are directing your writing to a group of people, envision one person who represents the group. Address your writing to that person.**

Mind mapping engages all of your brain power...

STEP 4: You are now ready to list the ideas associated with your topic statement.
To do so, you must brainstorm with yourself. Let your mind roam, freely associating ideas. This process allows you to cluster ideas creatively as they occur to you without worrying about neatness, style or spelling. Your goal is to provide some main ideas as well as details and examples to support them.

As you get ideas, write them around the core statement (Figure C). Work on both sides of the core statement. In our example, we've put ideas related to the problem on the left side and possible solutions on the right side. Depending on your subject, you may use the right and left sides in different ways. In a memo on a proposed procedure, you might list the pros on one side and the cons on another. For a report on a new product, you might group reasons for the product's development on one side and projections for its use on the other. Just be sure to determine some simple grouping based on your core idea.

> **Note: Although it is easier to use only two main headings when you mind-map, you may occasionally find it more efficient to use three or four. If, for example, you're writing about emergency office procedures, you might build your mind-mapping with three headings such as:**

1. **FIRE**

2. **TORNADO**

3. **BOMB SCARE**

As you mind-map, many of your initial ideas will lead you to related points or examples. Use lines to attach these secondary ideas to your initial ideas (Figure D). In Figure D, for example, "Tardiness hurts meetings" falls on the problem side. But the mind-mapper had additional thoughts about how tardiness hurts the meetings. Where did he put them? How did he organize them? If you study the mind-mapping illustration carefully, you'll see how each initial

Mind mapping expands, rather than narrows, your options...

idea branches into subtopics and then into other points or examples, much as a family tree goes from parent, to children, to grandchildren, to great-grandchildren.

As you record your ideas, it is important to work quickly enough to prevent your brain's logical side from interfering with its creative side. Don't be too critical. Don't eliminate any ideas at this point. Don't worry about spelling, punctuation, or grammar.

NOTES

Figure B

Write your target audience beneath the core idea.

Figure C

Write ideas around the core statement.

Figure D

*Attach secondary ideas
to your initial ones*

The Outline

Once you have your ideas on paper, you are ready to write an informal outline. You'll learn how to do this by following steps 5-7. By keeping the outline informal, you can forget all those horrid outlining rules about Roman numerals and parallel structure that you learned in school. Think of your outline as nothing more than a cheat sheet to help you organize your ideas before writing. No one else will ever see your outline, so don't worry about how it looks. Here is how you do it:

STEP 5: **Re-examine your ideas and decide which points are essential in stating your case. Mark them with a highlighter (Figure E).**

STEP 6: **On a fresh sheet of paper, list the highlighted points from Step #5 under the two or three major headings you used around your core idea (See "Problems" and "Solutions" in Figure F).** Leave plenty of space under each one. Then fill in the points you are using just as they appear on your mind-mapping (Figure F).

STEP 7: **Study the ideas you just listed under each topic.** You may want to change their order, putting the strongest points first. You can easily do this by numbering the points you feel are out of order (Figure G).

NOTES

Figure E

Highlight the essential points

Figure F

PEOPLE SHOWING UP LATE FOR MEETINGS

PROBLEMS	SOLUTIONS
40% OF STAFF LATE	SEND MEMO PRIOR TO MEETINGS
——— SOME LATE 30 MINUTES OR MORE	— GIVE TIME & LOCATIONS
	— SET AGENDA & SCHEDULE
TARDINESS HURTS MEETINGS	START MEETINGS PROMPTLY
— INTERFERES W/ ORGANIZATION	STICK TO SCHEDULE
— DISRUPTS COMMUNICATION	
STRONG COMPETITION	COUNSEL LATE ARRIVALS
— JOBS JEPERDIZED	— PUNISH FREQUENT OFFENDERS
DISRUPTED MEETINGS HURT WORK EFFORT	ASSESS CHANGES
— GOALS & METHODS UNCLEAR	— MAKE ADDITIONAL CHANGES AS NEEDED
— COMMUNICATION & TEAMWORK HINDERED	CALL TO ACTION
— PRODUCTION 50% SHORT OF QUARTERLY GOALS	— REQUEST CONFERENCE
— QUALITY LOWERED	. W/IN 3 WORK DAYS
	. W/ SUPERVISOR
	. DISCUSS IMPLEMENTATION
	. DISCUSS PROBLEM
	. OFFER SOLUTIONS
	CHANGES IMPLEMENTED W/IN 10 WORKING DAYS

NOTES

Figure G

PEOPLE SHOWING UP LATE FOR MEETINGS

PROBLEMS	SOLUTIONS
* ① 40% OF STAFF LATE	SEND MEMO PRIOR TO MEETINGS
—— SOME LATE 30 MINUTES OR MORE	— GIVE TIME & LOCATIONS
	- SET AGENDA & SCHEDULE
② TARDINESS HURTS MEETINGS	START MEETINGS PROMPTLY
— INTERFERES W/ ORGANIZATION	STICK TO SCHEDULE
- DISRUPTS COMMUNICATION	
④ STRONG COMPETITION	COUNSEL LATE ARRIVALS
— JOBS JEPERDIZED	- PUNISH FREQUENT OFFENDERS
⑤ DISRUPTED MEETINGS HURT WORK EFFORT	ASSESS CHANGES
- GOALS & METHODS UNCLEAR	- MAKE ADDITIONAL CHANGES AS NEEDED
- COMMUNICATION & TEAMWORK HINDERED	CALL TO ACTION
- PRODUCTION 50% SHORT OF QUARTERLY GOALS	- REQUEST CONFERENCE
- QUALITY LOWERED	④ · W/IN 3 WORK DAYS
	① · W/ SUPERVISOR
	⑤ · DISCUSS IMPLEMENTATION
	② · DISCUSS PROBLEM
	③ · OFFER SOLUTIONS
	- CHANGES IMPLEMENTED W/IN 10 WORKING DAYS

NOTE: *Number only those points whose order you want to change.

You are now ready to write. Your logical side is probably telling you to write clearly and logically, to be well organized and to be mechanically correct with spelling, punctuation and grammar. Don't listen! That's probably what you've been trying to do — and it hasn't gotten you very far, has it?

You're now ahead of the game because you know that whenever you put too much logic into the early stages of writing, your creative side, feeling neglected, quits. The flow of ideas, as well as the words to express them, dries up.

So, for the time being, forget about logic and concentrate on simply getting your words on paper.

The Writing

STEP 8: Begin with the first draft. Write as rapidly as possible, taking each idea in numerical order directly from your outline. Don't worry about grammar, introductions, conclusions or exactly how you say something. Doing so will stifle your creativity and hinder the most difficult part of writing — putting words on paper. The trick is first to get everything down (Figure H).

> **Tip: As a rule, if you are writing shorter pieces (letters, memos, brief reports), each of the main ideas serves as a paragraph. If you are working on longer documents (training programs, manuals, books or lengthy reports), each idea can serve as a heading or chapter title.**

The trick is getting everything down...

As you write this draft, you'll probably feel uneasy. That's understandable because you know that logic, organization, clarity and correctness are crucial to effective writing. But they come later. Right now your goal is to put all other considerations aside in favor of speed.

TIP: Think of this step as popping corn. You are taking the kernels of ideas from your outline and popping those ideas onto the page. If you stop to examine each individual kernel as it pops, some kernels will never pop and others will burn. Your goal is to pop the whole batch before you worry about how much you want.

Figure H - First Draft

To: Supervisor

From: Jane Smith

Re: Showing Up Late For Meetings

40% of our staff has been coming late to meetings, some 30 minutes or more late. Tardiness hurts our meetings, interferes with meeting organization and disrupts communication. Disrupted meetings hurt the work effort. Goals and methods are unclear. Communication and team work are hindered. Production is 50% short of quarterly goals and quality is lowered in a highly competitve market we can't afford to disadvantage ourselves by allowing this problem to continue any longer. Jobs are in jeperdy.

Here are some possible solutions

- Send a memo prior to meeting to set the agenda and schedule and gives its time and location.
- Start the meeting promptly and stick to its schedule.
- Counsel the late arrivals
- Punish frequent offendres
- Assess changes and make further changes as needed

As a call to action, I am going to request a conference for discussing the problem and offer solutions to be held within three workdays and that changes be implemented within 10 work days.

STEP 9: Now is the time to examine your writing more critically. Look for major changes you want to make. Answer the following questions:

- Do I have an introduction, a body and a conclusion? The introduction should include some form of the topic statement. The body should state the problems and suggest solutions. The conclusion should be some kind of call to action.
- Have I organized my writing by paragraphs that follow the major divisions of my out line?
- Are all of my sentences complete?
- Should I reword any sentences or change any words to make my writing clearer or more organized?
- Have I misspelled any words?

It will probably help to read what you've written to yourself. Your own familiarity with the English language will serve as a simple guide that will tell you if something doesn't sound right.

> **TIP: Think of the first draft as moving day. All you care about is getting every thing into the home. The second draft is like the second day. Now you can stand back, see what works and begin to rearrange.**

Edit with a red pen so you can easily spot your changes (Figure I). The comments in black explain the reasons for the changes. Then rewrite on a fresh sheet of paper (Figure J).

Figure I - First Draft Edited

To: Supervisor

From: Jane Smith

MORE DIRECT
FEWER WORDS

Re: ~~Showing Up Late For~~ Meetings
TARDINESS AT

INTRO - USE TOPIC STATEMENT

MANY PEOPLE HAVE BEEN COMING LATE TO MEETINGS. DURING THE
LAST PERIOD, 40% of our staff has been coming late ~~to meetings~~, some
BY AS MUCH AS 30 minutes or more late. Tardiness ~~hurts our meetings~~, inter-

feres with meeting organization and disrupts communication.
Disrupted meetings hurt the work effort. Goals and methods ~~are~~ *REMAIN*
unclear. Communication and team work are hindered. *AS A RESULT,* Production
is 50% short of quarterly goals and quality is lowered. In a
highly competitve market, we can't ~~afford to disadvantage our-~~
~~selves~~ by allow~~ing~~ this problem to continue ~~any longer~~. Jobs *WILL*
BE ~~are~~ in ~~jeperdy~~. *JEOPARDY (SP)* *OR OUR*

BODY = PROBLEMS & SOLUTIONS

Here are some possible solutions
- Send a memo prior to meeting ~~to~~ set the agenda and *EACH* *WHICH*
  schedule and gives ~~its~~ time and location. *THE MEETING*
- Start the meeting promptly and stick to ~~its~~ schedule. *THIS*
- Counsel the late arrivals
- Punish frequent ~~offendres~~ *TARDINESS*
- Assess changes and make further changes as needed. *THE IMPACT OF*

~~As a call to action, I am going to request a conference for~~
~~discussing the problem and offer solutions to be held within~~
~~three workdays and that changes be implemented within 10 work~~
~~days.~~ *TO IMPLEMENT THESE REMEDIES, I WOULD THEREFORE LIKE*
CHANGED FOR CLARITY *TO MEET WITH YOU WITHIN THE NEXT THREE WORK DAYS TO*
DISCUSS THE PROBLEM AND OFFER SOLUTIONS. I HOPE TO SEE
OUR CHANGES IMPLEMENTED WITHIN TEN WORKDAYS.

CONCLUSION - CALL TO ACTION

Figure J - Second Draft

To: Supervisor

From: Jane Smith

Re: Tardiness at Meetings

Many people have been coming late to meetings. During the last period, 40% of staff has been late, some by as much as 30 minutes or more.

Tardiness interferes with meeting organization and disrupts communication. Disrupted meetings hurt the work effort. Goals and methods remain unclear. Communication and teamwork are hindered. As a result, production is 50% short of quarterly goals and quality is lowered. In a highly competatitve market, we can't allow this problem to continue or our jobs are in jeopardy. Here are some solutions:

- Send a memo prior to each meeting which sets the agenda and schedule, and gives the meeting time and location.
- Start the meeting promptly and stick to the schedule.
- Counsel the late arrivals.
- Punish frequent tardiness.
- Assess the impact of changes and make further changes as needed.

To implement these remedies, I would therefore like to meet with you within the next three work days to discuss the problem and offer solutions. I hope to see our changes implemented within ten workdays.

STEP 10: Concentrate on the writing's

impact. Now you are looking for more subtle changes. Answer the following questions:

- Did I say what I meant to say, and did I say it clearly enough that it can't be misunderstood?
- What impact will it have on the reader? Effective writing must persuade others, whether you are trying to convert someone to your viewpoint or simply convince the reader that the information you present is accurate and credible.

To enhance persuasiveness, keep your writing short and to the point. If you are long-winded, you run the risk of losing your reader. Make sure that your sentences and paragraphs are short and that you eliminate any unnecessary words.

- Now that I have an introduction (Figure J), will it grab the reader? In our example, the introduction: "Many people have been coming late to meetings," is dull. It's more effective to say: "In the first quarter, production fell 50%. How much of that stems from poorly run meetings?" Note the change in Figure K.
- Did I appeal to the reader's natural self-interest? Put yourself in your reader's shoes.

The reader must benefit in some way from what you've written, even if that benefit is as simple as new information the reader needs.

Again, work with the red pen (Figure K), and then write your final draft (Figure L).

Figure K - Second Draft Edited

To: Supervisor

From: Jane Smith

Re: Tardiness at Meetings

MUCH LIVELIER INTRODUCTION

IN THE FIRST QUARTER, PRODUCTION FELL 50%. HOW MUCH OF THAT STEMS FROM POORLY RUN MEETINGS?

FEWER WORDS, MORE PRECISE →

~~Many people have been coming late to meetings.~~ During the ~~l~~ast period, 40% of staff ~~has been~~ late, some by as much *QUARTER* *ARRIVED* as 30 minutes or more. *← SHORTER, STRONGER*

EFFECTIVE ADJECTIVE ADDS TO PERSUASIVENESS *RAMPART* ↑

~~T~~ardiness interferes with meeting organization and disrupts communication. Disrupted meetings hurt ~~the~~ work effort. *OUR ← MORE PERSONAL, APPEAL TO SELF.*

THEY LEAVE ↑ Goals and methods ~~rema~~in unclear. *WHILE HINDERING* Communication and teamwork ~~are hindered.~~ As a result, ~~production is 50% short of quar-~~ *ALREADY USED, DON'T REPEAT* *HAS SUFFERED* *OUR*

USE SHORT PARAGRAPHS ~~terly goals and~~ quality ~~is lowered.~~ In a highly competatitve *WILL BE* market, we can't allow this problem to continue or our jobs ~~are~~ in jeopardy. Here are some solutions:

CORRECT TENSE

CLEARER STRUCTURE

• Send a memo ~~prior~~ to each meeting ~~which~~ sets the *BEFORE* *TO* *FEWER WORDS* agenda ~~and~~ schedule, ~~and gives the meeting~~ time and location.

• Start ~~the~~ meeting promptly and stick to the schedule. *EACH*

• Counsel ~~the late arrivals.~~ *OFFENDERS* *← FEWER WORDS*

• Punish frequent tardiness.

• Assess the ~~impact~~ of changes and ~~make further changes~~ *MODIFY THEM* *← FEWER WORDS* as needed.

~~To implement these remedies,~~ I would ~~therefore~~ like to *NOT NECESSARY* meet with you within the next three work days to discuss the problem and offer solutions. I hope to see our changes implemented within ten workdays.

41

Figure L - Final Draft

To: Supervisor

From: Jane Smith

Re: Tardiness at Meetings

In the first quarter, production fell 50%. How much of that stems from poorly run meetings?

Last quarter, 40% of our staff arrived late, some by as much as 30 minutes or more.

Rampant tardiness interferes with meeting organization and disrupts communication. Disrupted meetings hurt our work effort. They leave goals and methods unclear while hindering communication and teamwork. As a result, quality has suffered.

In our highly competitive market, we can't allow this problem to continue or our jobs will be in jeopardy.

Here are some remedies:

- Send a memo before each meeting to set the agenda, schedule, time and location.
- Start each meeting promptly and stick to the schedule.
- Counsel offenders.
- Punish frequent tardiness.
- Assess the changes and modify them as needed.

I would like to meet with you within the next three workdays to discuss the problem and offer solutions. I hope to see our changes implemented within ten workdays.

Summary

Although these steps may at first seem a long, tedious approach to memo writing, try to remember the first time you tied your shoelaces alone or learned to drive a car. Initially, the steps seemed never-ending and overwhelming. It seemed to take forever before you looped the lace or departed from your driveway. But once you mastered the steps, they became habits.

These ten simple writing steps work the same way. It may take an hour or more the first time you work a memo through using the steps. The next time it may take only half that. Then, before you know it, you'll be capturing your thoughts on everything without consciously stopping to ponder each individual step.

The best part is that the same principles apply to any kind of writing, from letters to lengthy reports to full-length books.

If you're overwhelmed by the seemingly giant leap from writing a memo to writing a book, keep this in mind: There is no question a book takes longer than a memo to write. You will need more information and will probably have to do more research. You may have more main points on your mind-map. Or you may create a separate mind-map for each major division of your work. Obviously, there will be more writing to do. But the actual process is basically the same. Once you've mastered that process, you can save an hour writing a memo — and days, weeks and even months writing a book.

Remember:

1) Think about your reason for writing.
2) Write your core idea or topic statement on paper.
3) Determine your audience.
4) List your ideas.
5) Decide which points are most important and mark them.
6) List those important ideas under two or three main headings.
7) Rearrange your ideas according to importance under each heading.
8) Rapidly put all of your ideas down in a first draft.
9) Polish the first draft into a second draft, checking organization, paragraphing and clarity.
10) Create a final draft, this time paying attention to the impact your writing will have on the reader.

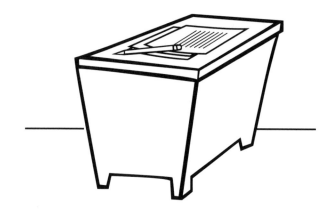

The Tips

If you've mastered these ten steps, you have enough information to write anything you want competently. But here are a few more practical writing tips to help you ease the process:

- If you're having trouble coming up with ideas during mind-mapping, you may not know enough about the topic. You'll gain confidence and knowledge by reading or interviewing people familiar with the topic. Your thoughts will then flow much more easily. It's a good idea, in fact, to do additional research at any stage you feel your ideas beginning to slow.

- If you're totally stalled after working for some time, take a break. Research shows that the subconscious functions during such breaks, drawing ideas together and providing new perspective. On longer projects, set the material aside for a day or two if you can. Not only does the break allow your material to incubate, it also gives your mind time to develop new perceptions.

- Don't expect too much from first or second drafts, especially on longer projects. Writing well is mostly a matter of rewriting.

- Don't try to write fancy. Most people do quite well when they write the same way they talk. The purpose of writing is to say something. If you communicate well when talking, there's no reason you shouldn't write the same way. Test your writing by reading it aloud to yourself. If it doesn't sound natural, rewrite until it does.

- It helps to have someone else read your piece and comment on it. Ask your reader if what you are saying is clear. An objective eye will often see flaws the writer misses.

- Don't be wordy. Use as few words as necessary to make your point. The simplest, shortest words are usually the most effective. Write short sentences and paragraphs that the reader can easily follow. Prune your work as much as possible without destroying its effect. Think of yourself as a word gardener who searches for written overgrowth and cuts it from the page.

  Start your word cutting by remembering a few simple guidelines:

  - Use possessives. Don't say "the report from the committee" or "the content of the report"; say "the committee's report" or "the report's content." You have already saved two words!
  - Avoid qualifiers such as "very" and "pretty." Don't say you are very interested or pretty interested; just say you are interested.
  - Don't use more than one word to say the same thing. Don't say "descend down"; say "descend." Don't say "I thought to myself"; say "I thought."
  - Cut phrases to words. Don't say "his work in the office is beyond reproach"; say "his office work is beyond reproach;" Don't say "the person who runs the accounting department"; say "the accounting department manager."

- Use the active voice, not the passive. In other words, never say that something was done by someone. ("The holiday party was planned by David.") It is better to change the sentence to the active voice by saying: "David planned the holiday party." Active voice takes fewer words and makes your writing more effective.

- Be sure that each paragragh includes a sentence that summerizes the paragraph's content. Every point in the paragraph should relate directly to that topic sentence. The sentence may go any-where in the paragragh, but you may find it easiest to start with the topic sentence. This is not difficult to do if you write directly from the outline you created in steps 5 through 7.

- Be sure you understand your audience. How much does your audience know about the topic? This will determine how much background information you must provide. Also consider your audience's sophistication level, vested interests and political sensitivities. In other words, if you were preparing a report on a major accounting error under your supervision, your written approach would depend on whether you were addressing the chief accountant, the com-pany president, stockholders or the general public.

- The steps in this book provide a framework for simplifying the writing process. Once you are familiar with our methods, feel free to experi-ment. Use what works for you!

- Don't take the rules of grammar as you learned them too seriously. They seriously confuse and intimidate. Over the last four decades, many of the rules have been relaxed, so you can do nicely with what you already know and a little common sense coupled with the grammar guidelines that follow.

For too many people, grammar is an intimidating subject. It shouldn't be. Although hundreds of rules fill the grammar books, the most common errors fall into a relatively small number of categories.

By mastering the few simple rules in this section, you will avoid the errors that are most distracting to the reader and you will gain the command of grammar that you need for confident, competent writing.

Grammar

First take this quiz

Fill in the blank:

1. That's between you and **(I/me)**.
2. Your objections to our proposal **(need/needs)** more clarification.
3. When **(your/you're)** done, please return each file to **(its/it's)** proper place.
4. We received all three **(committees/ committees')** reports.
5. After I **(lay/lie)** the books down, I'm going to **(lay/lie)** down for a nap.

Punctuate:

6. I hope the new program the one that began last week is all we expect it to be.

Improve:

7. It's difficult to choose between them, they are both excellent options.
8. The company is having their best year.
9. You left the decision up to Jim and myself.
10. While working late at the office last night, two mice ran out from behind the desk.

Bonus:

11. I had **(less/fewer)** than ten items, so I got in the express lane.
12. **Only** Pat checked the bills./Pat **only** checked the bills/Pat checked **only** the bills. (Which sentence is correct?)

Answers

1. **That's between you and me.** Don't be afraid to use the word "me." "Me" is a perfectly good word, but most people — even the most highly educated — seem afraid to use it.

- Always use "me" after prepositions such as "between," "to," "with" and "for." ("Please give it to Larry and me." "I read the report you prepared for Amy and me.")

- Always use "me" when you are being acted upon. Use "I" when you are doing the acting. ("He told Larry and me he'd have the report by Friday." But "I told him I would read it within a week.")

NOTE: The most common confusion between "me" and "I" occurs when referring to two people ("Susan and I"/"Susan and me"). When you're not sure which is right, just drop the first name. (You would never say: "Please help I." Therefore, you'd say: "Please help Susan and me" instead of "Please help Susan and I.")

2. Your objections to our proposal need more clarification. In this sentence, it is the "objections" that need more clarification, not the "proposal." Since "objections" is plural, the verb that goes with it must also be plural.

> **Note: Why is "needs" correct in the following similar example? We can see by your objections that the proposal needs more clarification. Answer: The verb "needs" now goes with "proposal," a singular subject.**

3. When you're done, please return each file to its proper place. Try not to confuse "you're" with "your." Use "you're" when you mean "you are." Remember, the apostrophe makes up for the missing letter. Also, you must memorize the difference between "its" and "it's." In "it's", just as in "you're", the apostrophe replaces the missing letter. "It's," therefore, means "it is"; "its" is always possessive: "It's wonderful to find the new software accomplishing its mission."

4. We received all three committees' reports. You must use apostrophes to show possession. The rule is simple: If there is more than one person or thing that possesses something, use the plural of the word and add an apostrophe

after the last letter: "supervisors' badges," "speakers' topics." If an object belongs to one person or thing, use the singular and then add an **'s** at the end: "supervisor's badge," "speaker's topic." Be sure that the possessed item is written in the plural when necessary: "Employees' paychecks" not "Employees' paycheck" because you are talking about more than one paycheck.

> **Note: Remember that although "its" shows possession, it does not have an apostrophe. Don't worry about the grammar behind it. Just memorize it.**

5. After I lay the books down, I'm going to lie down for a nap.

"Lay" means to put or to place an object somewhere. "Lie" means to recline. Ask yourself whether you mean to put something down ("lay") or you mean to rest or stretch out ("lie").

> **NOTE: Remember that when you refer to putting something somewhere in the past tense, you should say: "I laid the book down." Or "She was laying the book down." When you're referring to a person reclining in the past, you should say: "I lay down." Or "She was lying down." This may take a bit of studying, but don't be discouraged. Think of all the doctors with years of post-college education who every day tell their patients to "Lay down!" when they really mean "Lie down!"**

6. **I hope the new program, the one that began last week, is all we expect it to be.** Forget all the comma rules. Practically speaking, you're not going to sit down and study all of the regulations now. If you want, pick up a grammar book and check the most common usages. Beyond that, when you read your work aloud, see where your voice pauses. If it's a short pause, use a comma. If it's a long pause, use a period. You'll be right far more often than you'll be wrong. (See next answer.)

7. **It's difficult to choose between them. They are both excellent options.** Know when a sentence ends and use a period. Never join two sentences with a comma. The rule you learned in grade school was that a sentence is complete once it has a subject and a verb. If you're not comfortable with that, read the sentence out loud. If your voice pauses for more than a second, you probably need a period there.

8. **The company is having its best year.** The company is singular, so you can't refer to it by using the plural possessive "their."

> **NOTE: Likewise, say: "All employees can bring their families to the picnic" because you are talking about more than one family. Do not say: "All employees can bring their family."**

9. You left the decision up to Jim and me.

Don't use "myself" when you mean "me." This may be the single most common grammatical mistake you'll see. In fact, as a general rule, the times you use "myself" are so limited, you can probably avoid using "myself" entirely.

> **NOTE: If you must use "myself," use it only to refer to another word in the sentence or for emphasis: "I hurt myself." "I did it all by myself."**

10. While I was working late at the office last night, two mice ran out from behind the desk.

The original sentence says that two mice were working late at night! Such an error is called a dangling modifier, which means that there is no word in the sentence that sensibly goes with the phrase ("while working late at the office") before it. Make sure any sentence you write cannot be misunderstood.

11. I had fewer than ten items, so I got in the express lane.

Despite what they say in grocery stores, always use "fewer" when the items you're referring to can be counted; use "less" when it is a quantity that can't be counted (fewer apples/less fruit, fewer holidays/less vacation time).

12. **All three are correct depending on what you want the sentence to mean!** The words "only," "just" and "even" should appear directly before the words or phrases described. In this example, placing "only" before Pat means that no one but Pat checked the bills. When you put "only" before "checked," it means Pat only checked the bills; she did nothing else to them. Finally, putting "only" before "the bills" means Pat checked only the bills; she didn't check anything else. See how changing the placement of "only" changes the meaning of the following sentence: "Only Brett suggested the sales staff wear hats." Your answers should include everything from Brett being the only one to suggest wearing hats to Brett proposing that the sales staff wear nothing but hats!

The bonus questions are easy grammatical points to learn, but few people know them. Master them, and you're sure to impress those who do.

Now that you've completed Unstuck For Words, *you can appreciate the equally important but totally distinct roles creativity and logic play in writing effectively. In some ways, writing competently is like using a funnel. To begin, you engage your creative side by tossing as many ideas as possible into the funnel's wide end. But as you move through mind-mapping, outlining, writing rough drafts and making final grammar checks, logic kicks in and your focus gradually narrows. Writing that goes through both ends of the funnel is writing that flows.*

NOTES

NOTES

Figure A

Write your core idea in the middle of a blank piece of paper.